To Wende

Thank you for being consistant! Your ministry has pushed me to start my own and that is amazing to me.

— The Transparent Church Girl

T. Tareé

Library of Congress Cataloging-In-Publication Data

INTRO

Have you ever felt like you were aimlessly searching for the evidence of God in your life? Has living as a believer ever felt empty? Have you ever felt silenced by your faith? Have you ever wished that "church folk" would just get real about things? If you answered yes to any of these questions #Let's Get Transparent is for you!

   T. Tanee' takes an honest approach to discipleship and shares her own stories to reveal God's hand in every situation. #Let's Get Transparent is a collection of reflections written over the span of two years. T. Tanee' affectionately refers to these reflections as transparencies. The transparencies were collected and published in no particular order, so you can read back to front, front to back, or however the spirit moves you! As you read please use the spaces for notes throughout to express your reactions, feelings, and thoughts.

   Through writing and sharing her experiences T. Tanee' has grown immensely spiritually, emotionally, and personally. It is her earnest prayer that her words and experiences help someone understand that God is there, even in their darkest times. That it is ok to experience the fulness of life and still love God. Most importantly she wants you all to know that it is vital to seek and define God for yourself.

   T. Tanee would like to dedicate this book to everyone that wasn't afraid to love and befriend a quiet church girl. To all the people who allowed her to show them love of God in her own unique way. Especially her angels; those who left their legacy of love and acceptance, who taught lessons without speaking. May you all continue to rest in peace and power. To my beautiful great grandmother Virginia Maddox, Mama Fleeta, My Pete: Still no wooden nickels!

THE

TRANSPARENT

CHURCH GIRL

Real Transparency Moment. I'm going to share a secret with you all. I've been running from God. For the last few months I've been avoiding intimacy with God. Those of you with or desiring a REAL relationship with the Lord may be asking, why would anyone avoid intimacy with God? Well, God's touch is POWERFUL, and it comes with a few things: conviction, accountability, instructions, etc. I knew once I had a real authentic encounter with God there was going to be some work to be done on my part afterwards. Frankly, I wasn't ready to get myself together. I didn't want God to confirm the things I already knew I needed to do, so I ran. Avoided real worship, avoided the people I knew God used to speak to me the most, cut my prayer time, and made all kinds of excuses. However, this morning I found myself in worship in the midst of my prayer time. I was alone, there was no music, no one was cheer leading or begging me to do anything (you can be your own worship leader). I'd prayed for my friends and family and then I touched on a relationship that I'd been struggling with and the Holy Spirit showed up. Those things: conviction, accountability, and instruction followed, but there is also so much love from God here. Even though I was running God kept me, he allowed me to come to him in my own way and time. It's a relationship that I am so thankful to have!

TRANSPARENT PERSONAL REFLECTIONS

We are all going through something. I could come every week and tell you all about another "problem" in my life, but that wouldn't solve anything. This morning a friend of mine messaged me. Her family is currently grieving, and her message led me to pray. There was nothing that I could physically do to help the situation. My heart strings started to pull, water came to my eyes, and the hugger I am wanted to give them all a big hug. However, I know the comfort of the holy spirit is greater than even my best hug, so I asked God to meet them where they were, give them peace and understanding, strengthen them in their time of weakness, and heal their broken hearts. Do you know the power a prayer for someone else holds? God has called us all to intercede on behalf of each other.

We could all spend our time petitioning God for ourselves, but can you imagine the blessings that will surround us once we learn to pray selflessly? Just think of the impact we could have if we all joined on one accord and prayed earnestly for one another. This week I challenge you all to ask God to strengthen you and fill you with the desire to pray for others and then try it! This thing is all about perspective. Your blessing is in being a blessing to someone else. Try not to focus on yourself and watch your situation change. I'm going to continue to pray for my friend and her family because I know how ugly grief can be, it's a process that I know they can make it through. 1 Corinthians 16:14

TRANSPARENT PERSONAL REFLECTIONS

I made it another seven days and that's something to celebrate right there. If you're wondering why I keep doing this, it's because I need to write. It's my God given gift that I don't use nearly enough, nor in the right way. Anyway, if you know me you know I wear a lot of Christian wear. Sweatshirts, t shirts, those type things designed around scripture or Christian themes. It's an expression of myself. Recently I ran across a new site called Faithful Chic and purchased a shirt that says, "your gossip is my testimony". I looked at the shirt for months before purchasing, but the first time I saw it I literally yelped. Last year was a TEST, not a pop quiz, it was like the SAT, MCAT, LSAT, GRE, and all parts of the GACE put together. From family to finance I went down through there. The whole time I felt like I was under a microscope and my life was being reported by all major news networks.

Needless to say, I isolated myself from everyone, ended friendships, and hid. Yep, there I was running and hiding (just like I explained a few weeks ago), but God strengthened me, coaxed me out of my shell, sent new friends who could truly relate, and showed me that only he could judge me. I'm sharing my story to let someone else know that even when you think that the world is talking ABOUT you God will still talk TO you, he will talk FOR you too. You aren't alone, you're in the only company that matters. Be still and know that God is with you. Allow the holy spirit to dwell right where you are until you're ready to emerge. I know it hurts and you're scared, but if I got through it you can too. Let their gossip be your testimony!

TRANSPARENT PERSONAL REFLECTIONS

Saturday morning, I got news that disturbed me to the core of my being. I was so disturbed I didn't sleep for two days. Has something ever disrupted your spirit so that you felt every emotion possible? I was thankful for the outcome of the situation, angry that it took place, hurting for my loved one, and honestly afraid. I mean I felt EVERYTHING. I had to find a way to ground myself. How could I show any support to my loved one who had experienced something so terrifying if I was a mess of emotions? So, I delved back into my studies and ran across II Corinthians 12:9 But he replied, "My gift of undeserved grace is all you need. My power is strongest when you are weak." So, if Christ keeps giving me his power, I will gladly brag about how weak I am." God's grace was already all over the situation. I understood then that there was no need for me to do or even really say anything. Sometimes you must surrender the urge to be in control, to try and fix, or even help. Sometimes we aren't strong enough. God's strength is made perfect in our weakness! Moving forward we are going to have to take our hands-off somethings, step back, we aren't supposed to touch some situations you may mess up God's power at work. Just be mindful even in the toughest situations God's grace is sufficient!

TRANSPARENT PERSONAL REFLECTIONS

God doesn't confirm anything that he hasn't birthed. If I didn't know this to be true you would not be reading this book. I knew that I was created to write at the age of 13. I was assigned a poetry project and I waited until literally the last minute to complete it. I had to turn it in next period and I quickly wrote some lame rhyming words about a purple flower. After I tossed that in the trash I thought to myself write about something no one knows. This is your chance to write about something you're not able to speak about. I wrote a poem "You Meant Something to Me" to my granddaddy Payton.

That thing you've always wanted to do, the one that pops into your mind when your turn over in your bed at night, the thing you tried years ago that didn't quite work out, but you can't get over it.... THAT'S YOUR GOD GIVEN PURPOSE! If you're still asking What happens to a dream deferred, no it doesn't dry up like a syrupy sweet it knags at you day and night until you make it happen. It's time to live our dreams, they don't just develop out of thin air. These are God given visions. Complete the task and bask in God's glory as ultimately you will be pleasing God by walking in your destiny. It's my time! Who's ready to join me?

TRANSPARENT PERSONAL REFLECTIONS

The Curse of Supposed. We hear it all the time, the way things are supposed to be. We are taught the way we are supposed to do things. We talk about the order in which things are supposed to happen. We dream about the way life is supposed to go. Supposed is the greatest disservice we could ever place on ourselves and each other!

Lately, I have felt downtrodden and beat up by life! The news has just been one tragedy after another for weeks now. My personal life seems to be under attack. I just can't get right. I'm not supposed to be here. I did everything I was supposed to do. I'm supposed to be seeing more growth and progress by now. The book is supposed to be written. The degree is supposed to be granted. The babies are supposed to be on the way. Life is supposed to be settling down. The career is supposed to be established. Supposed will drive you insane. Supposed is seemingly driving me in sane. So, I'm left to question is anything ever as it is supposed to be?

I'm talking to the church girls (boys) like myself, who followed all the rules. You felt confident that if you did as you were told, followed this seemingly mapped out trail in life, and didn't rock the boat too much that life would be ok. You were always referred to as "the good one". They said go to college so that you can graduate and have a career, yet you've ended up in a dead-end job with no upward mobility. They said don't bring home no babies out of wedlock, but you're looking 40 in the face and hosting your little cousin's fifth baby shower because every baby is a blessing. They said marry that girl and make her an honest woman, but she is cheating all over town. They said God First, then Family and everything else will fall in place, but there is nothing else to fall. You feel cheated out of life. I get it. You feel repressed by the rules. When you express these things to people they start quoting scripture to you. I know, you know Galatians 6:9 by heart, and you still grow weary.

I don't have any answers for you beloved. I pray that God build you up where you are feeling weak. I pray that you have the strength to carry on. I know that there are people that have never been in our shoes who look at you and say walk away from everything, but I know that you can't even comprehend that thought. I know that in your heart you truly want to live by those rules, no matter what. I pray that some way somehow life shows you the reward you deserve. I pray that you are celebrated just as you celebrate those who have willingly done wrong. I pray that all that is good comes your way. Most importantly, I pray that you find freedom from the constraints life has put on you. In Jesus' name, Amen.

TRANSPARENT PERSONAL REFLECTIONS

We are in the middle of Lent! Many of us have given up things, taken time to increase our study or prayer life, or just strengthen ourselves spiritually. This is my absolute FAVORITE time of the year. This season leading up to Resurrection Sunday aka Easter is truly a season of celebration. As a child, I described it as Christmas in Spring. I have beautiful memories of worship, fun, food, gifts, and family. Honestly, some of my most cherished family moments are memories of Easter's past. I love it! However, today while I was reflecting and praying, I thought back to where I was this time last year.

I was in a very ugly space. Depressed, unhappy with work and home life, unbalanced, thinking recklessly, broken and weak. My spirit was deteriorating, and I felt hopeless. People looked at me and thought well she's a newlywed, with a great new job and the world ahead of her. I was stumbling through a marriage that seemed doomed, working a job that made me a misfit, unable to effectively communicate my concerns with anyone. I was sinking fast in life. I felt like I was losing my mind, and nothing made sense. I knew I had to do something or I was going to self-destruct, so I found a counselor.

I started going to counseling once a week. I discussed my marriage, my family life, my job, my deepest insecurities. I learned that my counselor was a Christian, a preacher's daughter, and living with a dad dementia. JUST LIKE ME! It's taboo in my community to seek help beyond your pastor or your mama but talking to someone removed from my situation saved me. It amazed me how God placed in my life someone who had lived all the things that were trying to take me out. She could relate and after a few months I started to feel like myself again. Bless God!

This Lent season I challenge anyone who is on the edge to take the time to reach out and practice some self-care. God has given us so many resources, utilize them. I'm here if you need me and I love connecting people to the help they need. In a few weeks when we sing about the blood flowing to the lowest valley, I know it does, but remember that it also reaches to highest mountain. Allow love and the sacrifice of Christ to Resurrection your spirits again!

TRANSPARENT PERSONAL REFLECTIONS

Transparency Tuesday: I'm going through a transition, but I refuse to come out of this thing not having learned anything. I'm determined to come out on the other side better! I want people to look on in shock and wonder so I can tell them how God is amazing. Recently, I was reminded of a sermon I heard years ago. The preacher used the Dogwood tree as an example. Dogwoods, when in bloom, are beautiful. They're stout, but when in bloom they spread. In the winter, you will see the tree bare, with its limbs cut back. Honestly, they look horrible.

You'll wonder why they would do that to such a beautiful tree. The horticulturist knows that if the limbs are cut back at the right time, in blooming season the beautiful blossoms will spread and reach further. Be encouraged, beloved if you are going through a tough time, this is just your pruning season. Its uncomfortable, its hurts, you may feel downright ugly, but blooming season is coming and the true beauty, your true purpose, your blessing to the world will reach further because you withstood your pruning.

TRANSPARENT PERSONAL REFLECTIONS

I'm so excited to share my first reflection in this new space! I thought I was going to be able to truly stay away from writing transparencies for a month but that didn't happen lol. Well this is my first OFFICIAL transparency in 2017 and on my new page. It's a bit loaded, but as always rock with me!

I'm from Atlanta! I know that's not shocking to most of you, but it's a fact. Check the birth certificate, ask my mama them! I'm an ATL GIRL through and through, but I'm not much of a football fan. So, when the Falcons played a good season I was happy for them, but not overly ecstatic. My heart was with the city. I was ready to cheer for the home team, because it's the HOMETEAM and I would expect anyone else to do the same! If you don't (insert side eye here and understand I don't trust you lol) ...God still working on me and judgement.

When Sunday rolls around I'm legit excited, but I can't let anyone know because I'm not really a football fan and I don't plan on watching the game. As we all know in the first half we're up, so I'm locked in, lol yep Ms. I'm not watching is indeed watching. Between the television and Facebook, I'm having a good time. Around the end of the third quarter the game begins to take a turn and I start watching a movie because I hate suspense. I also notice something happening on my Facebook timeline. People (fans and non-fans) start talking about the Falcons and how they always tend to mess up at the end "I can't trust the Falcons until the fourth quarter" "they can't hold a lead" and I was like dang well they have messed up some good leads in the past. Y'all I was convicted so fast, God said so have you!

How many of us have been ahead of the game and blew it? You got off early, ran all your errands, started your dinner and should have done some things around the house, but instead you jumped on Facebook or took a nap and messed around and got distracted.... you blew your lead! Or you were preparing to take that test for the certification that could lead to a raise, and you were studying well but you talked to someone who had the certification and they told you "oh, it easy, you got this" so you put your materials down and failed the test.... you blew it!

Remember that time you were praying, fasting, and trusting God for your breakthrough and you could feel your spirit being renewed, your situation was turning around, you got a step ahead in life and thought you could do it all on your own and forgot where your help was coming from...baby you blew your lead! How quick are we to react and give up on ourselves because we felt like we were ahead of things? When we blow our lead, it's disappointing. I was hurt for the Falcons and my city but reminded that I've done the same thing in life.

We must continue to encourage ourselves even when we are ahead, keep pushing. So many people were rooting for the Falcons, but they didn't REALLY believe in them, they're support came with a clause. Thank God, his support doesn't come with a clause. I'll bless you if you're still up in the fourth quarter if that was the case none of us would make it lol. Cheer the full game and the outcome may be different. Sometimes disappointments come, but I'll leave you all with this thought "if I'd never been let down I would have never ended up at the feet of Jesus".

TRANSPARENT PERSONAL REFLECTIONS

I'm blessed to be here and so are you. Everyday my spirit is renewed and I'm thankful. Through fasting and prayer, I wake up every morning feeling refreshed and I appreciate that because my days have been rough lately. Yesterday an old friend who'd noticeably been away from social media for a year shared that she been dealing with LIFE. She lost her job (career position), her relationship ended, her mom got sick. She was feeling low and had to step away. Her transparency reminded me of this time (March) 2015 where I was dealing with life. I felt like everything was crumbling. I was failing at life. I lost my job, my new marriage, a few of my closest friends, I was dealing with my dad's illness...everything came at me at once.

This was a defining moment in my life. Was I going to live or die? I wanted to die! I prayed to die! The only thing that kept me from hurting myself was the thought of causing my parents and grandmothers pain. Daddy was dealing with enough, how would they explain me being gone to him? At the time, I couldn't articulate my feelings. I'd never been more disappointed in myself. Honestly, you all, I don't know what turned me around. I've got some angels in my life and a host of folks that can get a prayer through. I remember laying on the floor one day. I was so depressed I was in physical pain and asking God to help me.

If you are reading this and you are in a similar position, if you don't think you can get any lower, if it hurts like hell; I understand. If you can't stand to look in the mirror (I wept every time I looked at myself) I love you! If you don't feel like you have anything else to give, your testimony on the other side of this will save someone's life. Take your time, but I know you'll get through it, you can get up, you're worth it!!!! We must stop acting as if life is supposed to be perfect, people that love the Lord have ugly days too. They don't want to hear scripture they want to see your heart. Go show someone your heart today. It may heal you as much as it helps them.

TRANSPARENT PERSONAL REFLECTIONS

Being a Christian Church Girl I've been taught to reverence the cross. In Christianity, the cross is a symbol of our salvation, our faith, and our strength. Yesterday I was deep in prayer and when I finished my spirit whispered, "there's a cross for everyone and there's a cross for me". Well, that stirred within me and I said Amen. A little while later I had to clean up a big mess for my dad and right before I started to call someone and complain my spirit whispered again "Must Jesus bear the cross alone and all the world go free?". Deep sigh! At this point I chuckled because clearly God was speaking. It was ironic that this hymn bubbled up in my spirit. First, I HATED devotion growing up! I absolutely loathed it and felt it was the biggest waste of time. I may or may not have cheered when my church service did away with it and decidedly arrived late when they brought it back lol. However, those hymns and prayers are buried in my heart now and they surface when I need them the most. Secondly, as we acknowledge this Lenten Season I'm learning we all have our crosses, we all have our path to Calvary. The question is will you accept your cross, will you make your way to Calvary, will you acknowledge your personal Simon (if you don't know who that is look up Simon of Cyrene)? Think about it. Are you carrying something that seems too heavy? Is there purpose in that burden? Do you feel crucified by the very people you are trying to save? There is great responsibility in following Jesus and it comes in many forms. As always, be prayerful and get transparent.

TRANSPARENT PERSONAL REFLECTIONS

When I was very young my brother had a pet hermit crab. I have fuzzy memories of its cage, the sand, and there was always an empty shell in the corner. He had this crab before I started going to school so I could have only been three or four years old, but it was intriguing in the way curious toddlers are intrigued by things lol. I never bothered it, but I watched it every chance I got! If you know anything about hermit crabs you know they change shells, this is called molting. A lot of animal's molt when they grow. When molting, hermit crabs come out of their original shells and for a moment they can't move. I discovered that this temporary paralysis is for their "skin" to slightly harden as a means of protection until they are safely into their new shell. Can you imagine how tight it must be for the crab as it outgrows its shell?

We go through similar transitions as we grow. First, we realize that it is time to move on. We become very uncomfortable. It may be painful to leave that job, that church, that state, familiarity, childish things, friends, a sense of comfort...behind, but it's necessary! After shaking our shell, we may be unable to move for a moment. Fear of the unknown, looking for the perfect new situation...this is when God protects and guides us. We are often vulnerable, raw, or sensitive in the midst of our transition. Finally, we, like the hermit crab, find the perfect new home!

Listen, growth is uncomfortable, it's difficult, and many of us are afraid of the changes that growth includes. However, only dead things stop growing! God wants to bless you with new experiences and new opportunities. He wants to bring new people, places, and things into your life, but you can't experience those things in an old shell. Jesus shared a parable about new wine never being poured into old wine skins. The old skins are weak and unable to hold the new wine, they burst. You can't receive the new blessings God has in store for you if you are resistant to change and growth! Allow yourself to stretch out in the fullness of all God has for you! Remember that a diamond is made from pressure, an uncomfortable situation. A pearl is created in the mouth of an agitated oyster, an uncomfortable situation. Your greatness may have to be polished by an uncomfortable situation...are you willing change your situation for the sake of your growth?

TRANSPARENT PERSONAL REFLECTIONS

If you live in the Metro Atlanta, you know that last Thursday was chaotic to say the least! Between shootings on highways, major expressways with bridges collapsing, and terrible storms coming through there was ALOT going on. I live east of the city and the storms knocked our power out at about 8:00 Thursday evening. Well, my phone wasn't charged, my nephews were on 10, and I couldn't get in touch with my husband. It was just too early for our home to be this dark! I tried to read, on the little juice my phone had. I lit all my candles (I love 3-wicks). I tried to sit and talk with my mom and the boys for a little while. Oh, and of course, I hadn't had anything to eat yet, so I was hungry!

Like I said there was a lot going on. I finally gave up my front around 10:30 and went to bed, but I couldn't sleep a wink. I tossed and turned, I'm in ketosis so I was hot, sweaty, and uncomfortable, but my biggest issue was quieting my mind. Thursday night I realized I'd been avoiding myself for a few weeks and this was the point of reckoning! When you need to sit down, God will find anyway to sit you down. I used to be very good a sketching out regular quiet time. I started meditating at about 9 years old. I've always understood the importance of quieting myself, but it was the last thing I wanted to do last week because I'd been suppressing somethings. Friday was my late great grandma's birthday.

While I was happy to celebrate the life she lived, it is very hard for me every year because she loved her birthday and I have great memories of celebrating with her. I was sent into a moment of grief Thursday night. In the middle of the dark, with no distractions (phone, tv, books, paper and pen) I was forced to deal with my thoughts, feelings, and emotions. I was forced to call on the Holy Spirit for comfort. I was forced to deal with my stuff! I used to talk about my friends that never sat still, that were always busy and couldn't stand to be alone. I used to say what are you running from, eventually you're going to face it or its going to face you. I'm sharing just to remind you all to take time and unpack yourselves, that stuff that you don't want to deal with, those feelings that you're trying to ignore, that situation you don't want to confront, or those dates on the calendar that you would rather skip over.... all of that will never disappear.

Be gentle with yourself. Allow yourself to deal with whatever it is you may need to deal with. I was a little upset at myself for getting so upset, how much sense does that make, but I've learned something about grief. Its displaced love looking for somewhere to go. After the wonderful 20 years I spent with my great grandmother I have a lot of love wondering. I tell people all the time I will have great grands of my own and still be missing my great grandma. In the next week, I want you all to take some time and remove the distractions, get alone, and spend some time with yourself. You'll be surprised at the things that come up and out.

TRANSPARENT PERSONAL REFLECTIONS

As you all know we are in Holy Week. This week closes out the Lenten Season and leads us to Resurrection Sunday affectionately known to some as Easter! *sings* It's the most wonderful time of the year lol. This is indeed my favorite week, this is the week when the body of Christ really flexes its muscles and comes together. I'm often reminded during Holy Week why I, personally, decided to follow Jesus!

That decision still excites me. 16 years later that decision is revealing itself with my purpose more and more every day. I thank God for that!!! I usually use the Lenten Season to increase my study time, which usually means I find a good devotional to follow. Over the years, I've found some dynamic and enriching teachings, but this year I just couldn't find one 41 days long that resonated with me. I did however, do a 7-day devotion by Tamela Mann that I enjoyed. Being unable to find a devotion that fit, I struck out alone to do some extensive studying of my own. I ran across some arguments as to how long Jesus' ministry lasted before his crucifixion.

Most scholars settled with 3 to 3 1/2 years as the book of John mentions three Passovers. Other theologians dispute this, but for the sake of our tribe lets got with 3. As a Christian, I have vowed to follow the teachings of someone who only taught three years. Now some may say, that crazy, and they do. However, I tend to look at it differently, how awesome do you have to be, how impactful do you have to be that your teachings cause people to model their lives after you after only teaching 3 years!!!! I'm thinking about something I've been doing for the last three years and its nothing for anyone to model themselves after.

We barely know what's going on lol, but Jesus was so dutiful and powerful in his purpose that he was able to change the world with his short ministry and his short life. Even in the last week of Lent I'm determined not to leave this season the same way I came into it. Going forth I want a renewed sense of purpose, I need God's strength and power to carry me! It's time to make an impact you all! This week ask God to reveal your purpose, ask God to equip you for change, ask for a renewed spirit and a refreshed focus! All things are possible, be encouraged. This week I'll be taking prayer request, if you would like prayer or would like to pray with and for me feel free to message The Transparent Church Girl there is a button up top!

Allow me a moment to thank God. Today is my father's birthday!!! I woke up full of praise that God has graciously allowed my daddy to celebrate 57 years, on today. God is faithful, and he is definitely a keeper! Amen!!!!! I know that may read a bit churchy, but give me a pass, daddy is a preacher and I am The Transparent Church Girl for a reason lol

TRANSPARENT PERSONAL REFLECTIONS

Good Morning Good People! Hopped up outta beeeeed, turned my swag oooooon, took a look in the mirror and tried to be as real as possible with myself! Let's get transparent! I was prepared to do a Lent reflection because my the last 40 some odd days was full of lessons, but the world is feeling flipped, turned upside down in the last two days. The death of Mr. Godwin disturbed me to my core. Thankfully I did not watch the video.

I have no desire to ever see anyone lose their life, especially not in a senseless act displayed to the world like this. Just as disturbing was people's reaction to the way his family is choosing to grieve. As a Christian, in times of trouble, I have been taught to turn to God. Yes, I pray when I feel helpless, I pray when I am confused, I pray when I am troubled, I pray when I am in great pain and I have been comforted. I watched a live interview Mr. Godwin's children and grandchildren did on yesterday they soundly said, "if our father gave us nothing else he gave us a heart for Jesus, he taught us to love"! I cried because I have received the same gift from my parents and I cherish my faith. It is tried, tested, and true to me!

However, to learn that people are criticizing this family, during this time when they need the most support, is sickening. I don't live in a fairy tale where I believe everyone believes as I do. That's the beauty of this life! God gave us all a path to follow back to him, but we must learn to accept other's paths. However, we need to have compassion for one another. If that had been a Sikh, Buddhist, or even an atheist family would we be criticizing how they grieve? No, but because it's a Black Christian family, that's grounds for attack. It needs to stop! We are all on earth having the human experience. At our simplest form, we are human, and loss of life is losing regardless. We must be better! We must do better! We must love one another better!

TRANSPARENT PERSONAL REFLECTIONS

taps mic Are ya'll ready to get transparent?!!! *crowd goes wild*
It's Transparency Tuesday and I've got something to share.

I went to The Steeple Awards last weekend. I went with a good friend of mine and we had a nice time. NotKarltonBanks was the MC, he was hilarious as expected. Dottie Peoples, Crystal Rucker, and The Harvest Tabernacle Church of Lithonia, Ga were among the well deserving award recipients. I have no gripes about The Steeples. They are still developing, as this was only the second year, so things could have been more organized. Overall, I enjoyed myself. Now on to yall church folk!!!!!

Yall came out dressed to the nines you all looked lovely! I appreciate any opportunity to step out with your best foot forward, so I have no complaints there. However, we dress up our bodies without dressing our spirits. We hoop, holla, and run for absolutely no reason! We gotta stop the church show, its unbecoming. For example: Zacardi Cortez was a presenter. He came on stage to present his award and before he could announce the winner folks were screaming SING ZACARDI!!! Now don't get me wrong, I know this man to sing down a spirit. His anointing is powerful, but the spirit wasn't moving when these folks started putting on. They were cheerleading him to sing and he did, and then came the shenanigans.

I promise yall one lady would have threw her panties at him had we not physically been in a sanctuary. For a moment, I thought she had forgot. I'm not here to judge the authenticity of anyone's praise...if it is authentic. What I saw Saturday was something I've seen in worship settings for years. I'm sensitive to the Holy Spirit, even when it doesn't touch me, I know what

53

it looks and feels like when I'm in its presence....it wasn't there yet. Zarcardi sung, this is not to take away from his gift.

I think his voice is amazing. This is to address the playing. The spirit could have moved with genuine expectancy from the people in attendance. It was over the top and spirit squelching! Had there been any non-believers in the room, there may have been, they left calling us clowns have no more love for the Lord than they had when they arrived. By the time the spirit began to move most of the audience had left. Ministry goes beyond the pulpit. Our sincere worship is a form of ministry! When we genuinely bare our souls, lift of hands, leap and run in joy; that is a testament of God's goodness in our lives.

Church folks leave the act at the sanctuary door, let's get real about worship. It's turning people off and away and frankly, I'm tired of reading articles about the dying church and why millennials aren't getting out of bed for service. Exhibit A! #imjustbeingtransparent share your thoughts. If I'm wrong, fight me lol. If you've had an experience tell me about it.

TRANSPARENT PERSONAL REFLECTIONS

I'm back!!! I'm just going to jump right in. If you know anything about me you know that Erykah Badu is one of my favorite, if not my absolute favorite, artist. I think her art is pure, real, and let's face it she's a transparent girl after my own heart. Baduizm was released 20 years ago, this year. I remember the first time I heard On and On and realized I'd found my tribe! LOL my parents were like "I don't get it", our baby about to be a head wrap wearing, incent burning, ankh carrying Sistah Soljah. Well yall they called it, and it is so :).

I say all of that to explain I've been a fan for a long time and her old music speaks to me just as loud as it always has. I have referred to certain songs as gospel because she is indeed preaching...if we are willing to listen before we bob our heads. Last night I was listening to Bag Lady from her second studio album. I've listened to the song countless times, but last night the men in my life were on my heart. Past, present, and the two little one's I love to life. A lot of times we don't acknowledge the bag...gage the men around us are toting.

Bag Lady speaks directly to women, but fellas you've got to learn to let go of those things that you are carrying that are holding you back too. I once dated a guy that I adored. He was an amazing man of God, great son and brother, educated, good job, homeowner, beautiful spirit and personality, BUT he was carrying some real ugliness from his last relationship with him that enabled anything to blossom from what could have been a great connection. He was scarred (still is) and on a destructive path, trying to outrun the hurt. The thing was that pain wasn't going to go away. He could leave those bags on the other side of the world and they would greet him at his doorstep every time, until he decided to unpack them.

I still pray that he finds the time to do it. I speak a lot about my dad and my experience as his caregiver, but the truth is there is a core to his illness. My dad has dementia and PTSD. Naturally, people correlate this with his career as a soldier, but the truth is I believe my dad went into the service with PTSD. He holds some deep resentments about his childhood, that have scarred him. In his current state, I don't know if my father can let go of his bags, but it is my prayer that even during his illness that he is able release some of the things that have pained and disturbed him for so long. I could go on and discuss all the men I've loved and some of the men I've lost because of their bags, but we would be here all day.

Guys, especially my beautiful black men, confront your demons. We all have them. It doesn't make you less of a man to address your issues. In fact, I believe a free man is the most attractive thing in the world. This goes back generations yall. Some of these bags are encoded in our DNA. Our ancestors carried some of these bags across the Atlantic with them and we are still carrying them all these years later. We have been freed from the physical shackles, but we are still weighed down by the mental and emotional things that we do not know how to let go of. Trauma, if not addressed, eventually kills us.

It's a fight every day, and I know a lot of us weren't rightfully equipped to handle all that comes at us "I guess nobody ever told you all you must hold on to...", but it is life and once we admit that our load is heavy, we can start unpacking and addressing the issues that are burdening us. Eventually we will be able to live in the fullness of whom we were created to be. Think about it, sand bags are tied to objects and dropped to make them stop and stay in place. If you do not want to be stagnant in this life you must disconnect yourself from those bags to move forward. #get transparentaboutyourbag

TRANSPARENT PERSONAL REFLECTIONS

Grace and Peace good people. I want to send a huge thank you to all the new followers and to everyone that reached out to me and interacted with me concerning last week's transparency! I greatly appreciate the outpouring of support and those of you that were led to share your own experiences. THANK YOU! It's a heavy subject that a lot of people are not willing or able to address- our own issues and baggage-- but you all rocked with me and went there.

Today, I'm going right back to it. We acknowledge that we have bags to unpack, there are things that have been dormant within us that have left us stagnant. When traumatic things happen in our lives we stay right there, frozen in that space in time concerning that issue, until it is resolved. If you had a painful experience with your first love at 18, every time you deal with love and trying to love you are doing so as an 18-year-old until you fully address and heal whatever is paining you about your first romantic experience. If your daddy left when you were 10 and you vowed to never trust another man to be with you, you could be married with children still acting as a 10-year-old that cannot trust men.

How can you raise children and manage a household as a 10-year-old that doesn't trust their mate to help them and be there? It's impossible to do in a healthy manner, which in turn starts packing your children's baggage before they even have a chance. Does that make sense y'all? If we leave these issues unaddressed we pass them on to our off spring. It is no secret that I want children of my own in the next couple of years, but I refuse to allow the things that me and my husband struggle with sully the lives of the beautiful babies that God will give us.

We must unpack! I'm not telling you what I've heard or read, I'm telling you what I'm living. Often, I look at my mother and I bless God. I won't go into the details of the lineage, today, but I can honestly say I probably have more issues concerning my mom's daddy than she does lol. I don't know how she was able to experience all that their relationship went through and not harbor the residuals. She did the work! I don't know how or when and she may not either, but she doesn't carry that, and she definitely did not pass the issues on to us. It's a wonder and a testament to the power of forgiveness.

The first step in unpacking is forgiving yourself and others. This is probably the most difficult because we must stop pointing the finger. I watch a bit of reality tv and for some time I hated to see singer K. Michelle pop up because she was ALWAYS going to say one thing "YOU HURT ME"! If there was ever a confrontation that was guaranteed to come out of her mouth. It made my skin crawl because it was so off base. We must learn to turn "you hurt me" into I'm hurting! Take responsibility for your own pain so that you can control and end it. That's the second step of unpacking, becoming accountable.

Let's be real, waiting on someone else to heal you is like asking them to twist the knife in your back, again. An apology is never for the person in pain. So, if you just must confront the source of your pain be certain to leave the confrontation holding the handle of the knife (pain) yourself. If you are holding the pain yourself, you can hand it over to the Lord for healing. You can only take control of your pain by forgiving the person that hurt you. Remember an apology is for the person giving it.

Forgive them for yourself. I'm a Christian, an act of remembrance and worship in the Christian Church is taking Holy Communion, one of the most important steps before taking communion is self-examination. I'm not sure how serious other believers really are about this, but I've been taught my entire life that if you have any hatred in your heart, any strife with anyone, that you should not partake until forgiveness is given. You must forgive those that have done the wrong against you and ask forgiveness of those that you have wronged, including God. That's a lot of unpacking, when practiced whole heartedly, but you cannot sincerely worship if you're operating in hatred. Next week we are going to wrap up the steps needed to unpack our way to wholeness.

In the spirit of transparency, I'll simply say this. For about 10 years God took away my ability to write, other than academic pieces. It was painful for me to lose this gift because writing had been my lifeline throughout my adolescents. It wasn't until I hit what felt like rock bottom and totally gave my life over to God that I was able to express myself fully through the written word again. I had to start unpacking my crap to get back to this. I tell you all that The Transparent Church Girl was birthed from my pain and healing, just imagine the greatness God will rise from within you once you start unpacking that luggage that is weighing you down! In light and love.

TRANSPARENT PERSONAL REFLECTIONS

They say the third time's a charm so let's try this again and get transparent! I promise this won't be long. Today's the first Tuesday in June. June's a big month for me :). That is all I will say about that for now.

This past Sunday the Christian Church celebrated Pentecost or the coming of the Holy Spirit. I'm especially thankful for the Holy Spirit as I am certain that it sustains me. I wish more people would acknowledge the gift, but I guess Pentecost is kind of like Easter, people don't want to celebrate because they don't understand the gift was already given. ANYWAY, I'll come back to that soap box another day too.

Today, I'm going to wrap up this "rant" on unpacking our baggage. Thank you all for your responses and interaction, as always. I'm going to keep this simple. The Bible says in John 9:4 "We must work the works of Him who has sent Me while it is day; night is coming when no one can work". It is imperative that we let go of this baggage while we have the chance. Like I've explained some of these things that we are carrying aren't even our own, we been lugging these issues around for generations, passing them on to our children, and so on.

What if I told you that you were the last stop, you just have to LET IT GO! Put it down and be done with WHATEVER your it, your bag, your issue, your secret is! I tell people that I didn't have daddy issues, I have granddaddy issue. That's not entirely true, I've had my hang ups with my dad, but my relationships or lack of relationships with my granddads has given me great pause and pain over the years. This is the kicker, they probably had no idea! These were bags I picked up and carried all by myself. One of my grandfathers died about 20 years ago. It wasn't until I started dating my husband that I decided I could no longer hold on to whatever it was that I was carrying regarding my granddaddy.

My husband and I had a big fight about one of his friends and it dredged up almost 20 years of junk that I couldn't express as a child. The first time I ever picked up a pen and wrote a poem I wrote about my granddaddy Payton. He was special to me, but his passing created a void that I expected to be full for a long time. I was disappointed when I lost him, but the fact is he is gone. The sun had gone down on whatever could have been and never was. Why ,20 years later, was I still holding that bag? Ironically, around the same time that I came to this realization, my Big Daddy was gravely ill. During his illness and decline I think we both realized that we didn't know each other the way we wanted to.

Unbeknownst to my family I would visit him when I knew no one was at the hospital, when he was home I would sit in his room and talk to him. It was hard to get alone time with him once he was sick, but it was worth it. We could connect. We would talk about things that we had in common, that we had never acknowledged in over 20 years. We did the work while the sun was still up and when the sunset on that relationship I wished that I had had more time, but I was at peace. I could put those bags down and replace them with memories and promises I made to him.

Who would I be to tell you all to let go of the things that are holding you back, if I was still upset about my grand dads? If I were still blaming my shortcoming on them, could I seriously say I was being transparent? Who holds things against a dead man? A fool. It's time for us to stop blaming our bags for the things we don't like or the things we can't do. It's time out for the excuses. It's time for us to live in fullness and in truth. I'm The Transparent Church Girl and I had granddaddy issues, but I'm healing. Even though they are gone I thank God for my grandfather's, all their shortcomings and all their achievements because they inspire me to be a better woman and to leave behind LOVE as they did. Yall just remember to PACK LIGHT!

TRANSPARENT PERSONAL REFLECTIONS

I wasn't going to write today. I wrote on Sunday and I was like well you know...once a week or whatever. However, I feel so good today and God has so graciously given me this gift and desire so here I am! Today I want to charge you all for the rest of the week to make joy your priority. If nothing changed in your life from this day forward could you still smile? Could you muster up a thank you Lord? Would you still be able to bless the creator? Maybe I'm just full or maybe it's because I see my birthday on the horizon, or maybe I'm just crazy enough to thank God in the middle of my mess, but joy is one of my top priorities.

I find that joy by praising and thanking God. If you're in a place and you're like Church Girl, it sounds good and its easy for you, but nah sis I got bills piled up, a sick puppy, my toe hurt, I need a haircut, and pay day aint this week...I feel you! I've been there, but I dare you to say thank you Lord anyway. Our thank you's, our praise, our hallelujahs activate something and once that is activated things begin to change. You feel lighter and your frown becomes a smile. Sincere gratitude translates as joy and joy morphs into peace. If you are seeking your safe place, your calm in the storm, just open your mouth, your spirit, your heart, and begin to bless God.

I know it may sound crazy to some of you, but get alone somewhere (I use to be partial to my car, as that was once the only place I could be totally by myself) and just tell God that you want to make joy your priority, in spite of your circumstances, ask God to give you sight beyond your immediate situations and then say thank you even if that's all you can say. There will be those that try to kill your joy and dim your light, but when joy is one of your priorities you will find yourself deflecting them. You'll pick up on the negativity before you even encounter it. Try it out and let me know how it works for you all, it's been good for me!

TRANSPARENT PERSONAL REFLECTIONS

I'm The Transparent Church Girl and I'm here to confess that Pretty Church Girls love trap music too! Are you all willing to be my support group? Please understand I'm serious. Which is what led to all of this. Sunday, I went to a TI concert and had a decent time. I'm completely out of practice dealing with crowds. I still have terrible anxiety from being trampled at a party in college and blacking out, so my guard was up at the concert. None the less once I was able to establish my personal space (I don't play about it) I was able to enjoy the show.

TI did all his hits, Young Dro's set was LIFE, but surprisingly Two Chains (he will always be Tity Boi to me) popped up and did a few songs and that's when I came to this conclusion. Yep, standing in a crowded room full of white kids dry humping each other I, The Transparent Church Girl, admitted that Pretty Church Girls Love Trap Music! Now I know you're thinking why were you thinking about church while at this concert...you so saved lol. Well obviously,, I'm not the only one. I heard Jesus more at this concert than I've heard from some of your favorite gospel artist. That's another post for another day. Almost everyone that touch the stage Sunday took a moment to openly thank God for the opportunity.

As most of you know Two Chains just released his third album 'Pretty Girls Like Trap Music'. Everything from the music to the marketing is on point! He did it all right! So, it feels like this music I grew up dancing to and these artists that my friends had posted on their walls has really evolved. I know Jay Z told yall he was a business (man) years ago, but that didn't resonate with me. Sunday's show was a parade of home, people that claim Atlanta, that talk and walk Atlanta. People that remember Fulton Stadium, that can name city housing projects that transplants have never even heard of. It felt good, it felt familiar which is something Atlanta natives rarely get to feel these days.

However, the church girl in me would be remiss if I did not explain that you must guard your spirit. Trap Music is talking about being in the trap and all that comes along with it. I'm never trying to live that life, but I will sing along and dance. Just remember music is powerful. I'm just being transparent with you all.

TRANSPARENT PERSONAL REFLECTIONS

Last Friday was my birthday. I thoroughly enjoyed myself. Usually on my birthday I wake up in tears, overwhelmed by emotion. Thankful, regretful, fearful, excited, anxious.... all at once, so I cry lol. This year was a little different. I woke up feeling very serene with a smile. I simply felt blessed. In those first few moments of the day I wasn't focused on the past or the future, I was able to appreciate making it another year. As the day went on I thought of somethings that I've learned to be true as of late. Here we go...

1) GOD IS... - You can put pretty much anything behind that at this point.

2)Your biggest victories are defined by how you react to your biggest failures. How did you handle taking an L?

3) The church does not determine my relationship with the Lord

4) Church hurt is real for so many people. For years, I felt the need to defend "the church" instead of help heal the hurt.

5) Friendships aren't measured by time, they are measured by heart.

6) There is a such thing as putting too much pressure on yourself. You are not and never will be perfect.

7) If God has forgiven you why are you still struggling to forgive yourself.

8) People will use your relationship with Christ against you.

9) When people try to shame you for being selfish they are usually only thinking of themselves which means you both can't be selfish, and they want their way before you get yours.

10) I'm repelled by strong personalities. People that come off too strong or never show humility put out energy that I haven't learned how to navigate yet. When I say, people are too much I usually mean it.

11) For most of my life I thought I was Daria while the world saw Suzy Carmichael. True story lol. I didn't realize how bubbly I can be until the last couple years.

12)The closer you get to God, the clearer you will see who and what is around you.

13)Prayer changes things, but most importantly prayer changes you!

14) Anything that is broken is useless, even you! Find a way to mend.

15) Marriage is the hardest thing I've ever done. No one is honest about marriage.

16)If you are able and moved to help you always should. You never know when your upper hand could turn into a hand out.

17) Material things can certainly be replaced.

18)Sometimes you are going to be the only person cheering in the crowd. Don't stop! Eventually others will join in.

19) Grief comes in waves, you can't fight them, or you will drown.

20) When I (the Church Girl) believe in something I don't give up.

21) In life pain is inevitable, but healing is imperative.

22)Forgiveness is the key to freedom.

23)One of my favorite television theme songs says it best...Life Goes On.

24) If you don't find a way to relax you will self-destruct. If your only ways to relax include sex, drugs, drinking, and or partying...you will self-destruct.

25) Hurt people hurt people in ways they can't imagine for years they may never see.

26) Every once in a while, you just must dance or wiggle your toes in the sand.

27) After God's love, self-love is the only other love that matters.

28) When all you see in pain you lose sight of God.

29)When you pray for rain you can't be upset when there is mud.

30) As long as I'm seeking God I will never stop growing.

31) BONUS: A mother's love is always necessary, but all mothers aren't created equally.

This has been hard for me to accept. I have a really good mommy, but everyone isn't as lucky. #mindblown so happy to be here. Thank you all for taking time to read this week. I've got somethings up my sleeve. As always, I'm ready to #letsgettransparent

TRANSPARENT PERSONAL REFLECTIONS

I'm currently going through a process where I have to be completely transparent! There is literally no stone about my life left unturned. I haven't felt this vulnerable and exposed in a long time. On paper, when it's written out in its totality, my life looks a mess ya'll! The pieces of my puzzle haven't found their way all together yet. As I go through this process and have people interviewed about my most personal affairs I realize the blessing in being The Transparent Church Girl and being Tannisha Tanee. God's got me.

My faith has never been stronger than it is right now. My love for my family, my friends, humanity has never been stronger than it is right now and it's all because of the love and grace God has shown me. Every piece of my crazy puzzle has a purpose. My marriage has a purpose, my family is dealing with my father's illness for a purpose, I've lost and left 4 jobs in the last 2 years for a purpose! I write and give of myself each week because this is all a part of God's divine purpose for my life.

No, I can't wrap my life up in a pretty bow right now. No, my husband and I don't have a house with a picket fence right now. Yes, my resume looks like a hop scotch chalk outline, but I'm fuller than I've ever been. We must learn to let go of expectations and allow God to work. I promise you if you just stay faithful things may not always look the way we think they should, but God will give you contentment while he puts your puzzle together.

When I was young my mom was crafty lol so we put together a lot of poster puzzles. I remember I had a My Little Pony puzzle that I was excited about, but I was having a hard time putting it together. One of the

81

pieces had bent back so I didn't think it fit. I rearranged the puzzle a few times, I cried, I wanted this poster so bad. Eventually someone helped me, and they found the bent piece. They bent it back and put sealant on the back, so the piece would lay straight. Viola'! My puzzle was put together and I had the cutest My Little Pony Poster. There may be some frustrations in life, you may have to hand over the reins and be vulnerable at times, but the final picture will all be worth it. Amen!

TRANSPARENT PERSONAL REFLECTIONS

Tip Top of the day to you all! It's time to get transparent. The word tells us "the diligent find freedom in their work" so I'm back! First, I'd like to ask everyone that reads today's transparency to please take a moment and share it. You can do that by clicking share in the bottom right corner. I'd greatly appreciate that, this is helping to not only reach a larger audience but also collect data before making more moves for The Transparent Church Girl.

I was raised to be a private person. My mama was strict about not telling outsiders family business. Outsiders included family too. I spent the first half of my childhood away from my extended family while my daddy was in the Army so when we were home it was always smiles and reunions. At some point that rule was internalized, and I stopped verbalizing a lot of things that happened to me. That shut down then turned into lying. It became easier to say everything was great and smile then to be honest because no one wanted to hear the truth, or so I told myself.

I went through some of my hardest times with a fake smile. I smiled my way through, but my spirit was bound. When I did talk about things it was only scratching the surface because I wanted to help everyone else. I was used to being the listener and comforting others, but I often stifled myself. It wasn't until my marriage almost dissolved and I lost the few things I called my own that I realized it was time to talk or I was going to self-destruct. At this point I found a therapist and learned to share my truth. From there I grew to be transparent.

Last week someone asked me a peculiar question. It was unnecessary, but it came from one of my triggers. Triggers are people that you encounter, and they knowingly or unknowingly arouse visceral reactions from you. These are usually people that know how to push your buttons, although they don't always realize that they are pushing your buttons. I have a few family members that are triggers for me. You know that older aunt you avoid because she always tells you how fat you've gotten, which usually tailspins you into deep depression and a week of binge eating? Yes, she is one of your triggers. No, she won't realize she is hurting you with her comments and she will never apologize. You must find the strength in yourself to become bullet proof because she is always going pull that trigger.

I had taken habit to avoiding my trigger(s) all together. Some are much easier to side step than others, but last week I agreed to interact. Anyway, the question was asked and usually I admit I would have quickly lied and put on a smile, but I don't live like that anymore. This new leaf I've turned over reminds me that my work gives me freedom and regardless of my triggers response to the truth I was up to the challenge. Surprisingly there was no rebuttal, no further inquiry, no response lol. I was use to adjusting for everyone else's sake while struggling. My truth changed nothing in anyone else's life, but a lie caused turmoil in my own...while everyone else slept peacefully either way. Why put yourself through that?

I don't know who needs this, but free yourself! You're painting pretty pictures for everyone else while you're living in a personal hell that you are creating. You don't deserve it beloved. Paint the picture for yourself first, walk in your truth with your best foot forward. When your life looks beautiful through your eyes everyone else won't be able to help but to see it because you'll glow. They'll greet you and that aunt will say "baby you look so good" instead of commenting on how fat you are. You won't have to diet a day in your life. This is what the deacons mean when they sing about laying their burdens down.

Galatians explains "It is absolutely clear that God has called you to a free life. Just make sure that you don't use this freedom as an excuse to do whatever you want to do and destroy your freedom. Rather, use your freedom to serve one another in love; that's how freedom grows. For everything we know about God's Word is summed up in a single sentence: Love others as you love yourself. That's an act of true freedom. If you bite and ravage each other, watch out—in no time at all you will be annihilating each other, and where will your precious freedom be then?" I love this freedom too much to ever risk losing it again. So, I'm committed to sharing the truth and doing so in love. Join me on the journey! I know we all want to project what's ideal and simple, but the complicated beauty of the truth gives so much more. I challenge you all to walk in your truth! #letsgettransparent

TRANSPARENT PERSONAL REFLECTIONS

Somehow my entire morning transparency was lost. Anyway, I want you all to join me in saying HEEEEY AUGUST!! By the grace of God, we made it! Today we head into the 8th month of 2017. Now some people are going to say wow the year is just flying by, but baby I'm not going to front for you, I've felt every single month lol. August comes with the promise of renewal and I'm excited about it.

August is the 8th month of the year. The number 8 represents new beginnings. The number 7 is the number of completion. God created the heavens and the earth and rested on the 7th day because he was done. On the 8th day he released Adam into what he had created for him. Let's stay right here...what if God was ready to release you into whatever he has created specifically for you January-July? That's something to shout about. I mean I know I'm excitable, especially when it comes to the Lord, but just the thought of God caring enough about me to take the time and set up a situation just for me...WOW. After all the misfits, the denials, the disappointments, and rejection God is about to let me loose in the place he made just for ME!!!!

That's Amazing! Many of you have told me about your plans to get a new job, or interviews you've went on, trying to start a family, saving to buy a new house, or start a business...now is the time! Prepare yourself through prayer to walk into this new season. Begin your prayer by showing deference. My fellow Greeks probably cringed lol, but God deserves the honor! Let God know who he is to you in your life. Adore the Lord. Secondly, you want to go into confession of your sins. If you are going to ask God for anything you should first, ask for forgiveness. August cannot be a new beginning if we are still carrying old transgressions. If it is something you are struggling with, now is the time to ask God for help and strength.

Then in the spirit of expectancy thank God. There is so much to thank God for...just so much. Finally, after we thank God then should we petition God for our wants and needs on behalf of ourselves and others. Through intercession we converse with God. If you take a minute to yourself during this time you will begin to hear from the Lord. After this I usually repeat step three and close my prayer with more gratitude.

Walk into August with a spirit of expectancy. I feel great about the new things God is bringing my way (and yours). There will be significant growth and revitalization in this new season. If you believe God for your renewal in the month of August tell me about it.

TRANSPARENT PERSONAL REFLECTIONS

Over the last few weeks I've started a personal study of the book of Galatia. I can't tell you all how much this has blessed me. I learned that the book is a collection of letters written by Paul to some of the churches in Galatia. The book is full of direction and instruction. The letters were written to express the Apostle Paul's disappointment and correct the young churches. Although some scholars have said that the tone is harsh, I went in search of answers and found them.

I've been enlightened and even encouraged during my studies. In these letters, Paul points out that we are constantly battling between our spirit and our flesh. Coincidentally I heard a sermon on Sunday entitled "That's what I like" on the same subject. There is a sense duality in living life as a Christian. Yes, in Christ we become whole, but in my experience, there has been a quest for that wholeness.

I've been saved almost 20 years, naturally becoming a Christian at such a young age meant I had to grow naturally and spiritually at the same time. This growth didn't happen at the same rate. I finally feel my spirit filling out and coming into its own. Growth. I had to learn to feed my spirit. Just like my body performs differently when under an adapted diet, I'm learning that my spirit thrives under a certain diet as well. My spirit may not flourish on the same diet as someone else. I get asked all the time why I still attend the same church that I grew up in. It's simple, I'm still being fed there.

Being spiritually fed goes beyond sitting in church on Sunday mornings. We must take personal responsibility for our spiritual growth as well. On Sunday alone I heard three sermons, thanks to the internet I was able to worship in three different regions of the county and be fed. It's like eating physical food; spinach doesn't give you all the vitamins and nutrients you need so you need to diversify and round out your meal. When you start giving your body those different sources of nutrition it starts to crave them. The same thing happens with our spirits.

We start to crave spiritual nutrients. We start having personal bible studies (lol) I remember a time when I would have never done a personal study by myself. I may have read a chapter or two to follow up on Sunday's sermon if something caught my eye while I was supposed to be turning to my neighbor). We begin to engage ourselves in spiritual enrichment throughout the week. There is a yearning and a desire for more.

Ironically, as we begin to desire more for our spirits our flesh begins to falter. The other day I was talking to my best friend about the movie Girls Trip. I was excited to see the movie because I'd heard so much about it and "actor baes "Kofi Siriboe and Larenz Tate are in it!!! Well there is a scene where Kofi Siriboe runs out of the bathroom naked. Being the girls that we are (we've been friends longer than I've been saved so we can be real school girls together lol) she asked, "did you see Kofi", she was ready to giggle because she knows that would usually be met with giiiiiirl. However, my reaction was different. My flesh didn't react. Now, I'm not blind the man is gorgeous, but the scene and his character were simple and silly.

This is an example of my flesh fading. Some time ago she would have gotten that giiiiiirl and a whole lot more. That day my spirit won, but it does not always win. We must make a conscious effort to determine if we are

94

going to feed our spirit or our flesh. On Monday nights when I watch my Love and Hip Hop, that's all flesh lol. When we hop on the phone and call our friends for "the tea", that's all flesh. When you call that person, you said you weren't going to call anymore because y'all never end up in the right places...yep that flesh and it happens.

You must seek out alternatives. The more you feed your spirit, the more you'll want to and vice versus. The Message Bible Galatians 5:16-18 puts it like this "Live freely, animated and motivated by God's Spirit. Then you won't feed the compulsions of selfishness". Naturally we all live and follow our flesh, we give in to our desires, ever since we were babies. Now is the time to do things differently. If you want to see different results from life, have different experiences, set some time aside to feed your spirit, engage in some spiritual activities and stretch out in your spirit. Tell me how it works out for you. Let's get transparent! Grace and Peace

TRANSPARENT PERSONAL REFLECTIONS

Let's get transparent! For the past few weeks every time I opened my mouth or shared my thoughts someone took offense. No lie. I've gotten into it with some of everybody and it wasn't intentional. It seemed like I just could not say the right thing, so I took that as a sign from God that I needed to shut up! I've created this space to share my thoughts, words, voice, and testimony and many of you have shared with me how God has used this space to speak to you all.

I don't take that lightly and I would never want to sully this space with my foolish blunders. I share a lot of myself here, but most importantly I try to share, what I can, of God. It is my earnest prayer that God comes across organically and as purely as possible from such an impure being as me. Around the time of the big eclipse I started to notice that my words were not being received as I intended. I could say excuse me and people would say why you gotta be so nasty and have an attitude.

The simplest things were being taken the wrong way. So, I had to check myself, like God what's wrong with me? This is when people started coming to me say "church girl sometimes you just gotta shut up" "it's best to just say nothing at all" "well just don't respond" and I was like ok God, I'm going to shut up. I messed up a few things over the last few weeks before I finally got the message. God was like T. HUSH YOUR MOUTH! T. SHUT THE UP! The most ironic thing is, naturally, I don't talk that much.

I'm learning it wasn't my mouth that God was trying to get a hold of, it was my ear! Over these last few weeks I have been blessed by some amazing sermons. My church does Tuesday Noon Bible Study that I've been able to enjoy. I took more time to crack open my Bible and dig a little deeper with my studying. I shared a sermon series entitled "what's in your ear" and if you didn't take the time to check it out please do! I may have even strengthened some of my personal relationships because I simply listened with no rebuttal.

We all put our foot in our mouths from time to time, but when you start doing it time and time again it's time for some self-reflection. A lot of us are quick to blame everyone else. They so sensitive, they just stupid, they not cultured so they wouldn't understand, they just don't like me...NO you just running your mouth! Take a step back. I'm quick to call my best friends Falion and Chasity and say Hey, tell me if I'm tripping about xyz. Pull my coat tail if I'm wrong. I love them because they are ALWAYS 100 with me. They feel no type of way about saying YES, you are wrong! This time I didn't even call them because I was afraid my words wouldn't come out right to even my closest friends.

My husband was flat out done with me, so I couldn't go to him, he had gotten the worst of my twisted tongue. Every so often me and my mama can mince words, so I tried very hard to stay clear of her because I knew it was me. I had to cry out to God, God its ME and God simply said be still and close your mouth. I have so much to share with you all. I have some good discussion pieces, and testimonies, but first I had to be obedient.

Life and death are in the power of the tongue. I don't want to kill this great opportunity, this great ministry, that God is carving out for me by being out of order. I recently heard that God cannot heal what you won't reveal so in the spirit of transparency I had to share why I'd gotten quiet. Some of you may need to zip it too. God could be trying to tell you something, but you're so gassed on the sound of your own voice, your own complaining, your own bragging, your own berating that you miss it. Don't miss hearing from God, his voice is so much sweeter than anything we've ever heard because when God speaks to you it's a gift, accept it!

TRANSPARENT PERSONAL REFLECTIONS

I just finished writing out some big goals for the book and life coaching. The ball is rolling!!! It seems like the storm (Irma) has passed. Keep the South in your prayers, its hurricane season and another storm will be here in a few days. I had so much to talk to you all about, but this morning my heart is heavy. I decided to change today's transparency late last night because this topic can't be ignored. I was talking to my best friend about Kenneka Jenkins. Kenneka was found dead in a hotel freezer this past weekend, after partying with friends. She was only 19 years old. Like many people my friend got swept up in following the case.

There's a lot of information, videos, social media post, and things surrounding this case so naturally people are trying to piece the story together. My reaction was a little different. I immediately remembered the 19-year-old church girl. Last night I ran across a picture of her. She was smiling bright, cute as a button, hanging with her friends. The church girl always had a crew. Even when her longtime friends disappeared or let her down she rarely ever rolled alone. I had to give it to her, she was fly with her little haircut. As I looked at her picture I also recalled she partied from Thursday to Sunday weekly. Every party wasn't official, some were kickbacks. Some were out of town. Others were major city-wide events. 19-year-old TCG just wanted to have a good time, she wanted to feel the excitement in the air while everyone was desperately trying to be cool. She was there to see whatever boy it was that week. She loved men!

There was a constant game of cat and mouse going on with me. My only saving grace was that I didn't drink (under aged drinking happened all around me) and I wasn't into drugs. The dangers of everyone else being drunk, high, or both never crossed my mind. If the DJ was right (RIP Dyce Law or Southanbred) and my outfit was cute then I was going to have the time of my life. I was young and foolish because I wasn't always as aware of my surroundings as I should have been. When I heard Kenneka's story and looked back at myself at 19 years old I realized it could have been me.

Yes, today's young people are different. They do things that we will never understand. There is a lot of speculation surrounding this story right now. I can say this speaking for only myself; I know that I have been places I've had no business being. I've trusted stranger's way to easily. They say never trust a big butt and a smile, well that's never been my issue, but an educated black brother and a smile is kryptonite. As a kid, I was uptight, my brother and his friends would tease me and tell me to loosen up. As a young adult 19-20ish I went with almost anything to show that I wasn't uptight. That alone landed me in some situations that were better left unexplored.

I didn't know Kenneka Jenkins, but I did know a 19-year-old that just wanted to have a good time. My heart aches that this baby lost her life in the name of a good time. It turns my stomach that we feel we can't have a good time unless we got drugs and drank. It scares me that society has us so cold that no one in that hotel room has told the entire story yet. It pains me that these girls were on FB live while their friend went missing.

We're out of touch, but we're always plugged in! That's crazy! As The Transparent Church Girl I will say pray for Kenneka's family. Her mother gave her the car keys expecting her baby to come back home that night, that didn't happen. I'm supposed to also tell you all to pray for our youth, and you should, but more importantly I'm going to urge you to teach a youth to pray for him\herself. When you learn to go to God on your own behalf, you gain a sense of accountability for your actions. Once you build a relationship with God, you must answer to God. I should also tell you to take the time and talk to a young person, but rather than talking to a young person I charge you all to listen to a young person. It may take some work to get them to open up, but it's vital to their survival that we know what's going on with them.

I can tell them my story all day, but 10 years ago is already unrelatable to them. Yep they gone tell you you're old, ain't nobody listening to that anymore. So, tap into them and see where they are and build from there. It may not save everyone, but our babies are being lost, a generation is in the wilderness, and we can lead them back if we take the time to first find ourselves and then show them a better way. It's time to get transparent y'all, so much depends on it.

TRANSPARENT PERSONAL REFLECTIONS